Spiritual Biographies
FOR YOUNG READERS

Gandhi
India's Great Soul

Maura D. Shaw • Illustrations by Stephen Marchesi

Walking Together, Finding the Way
SKYLIGHT PATHS Publishing
Woodstock, Vermont

Who Was Mahatma Gandhi?

Mahatma Gandhi was strong, even though his body was thin and small. He was the leader of one of the largest countries in the world, but he never wore fancy clothes or lived in a presidential palace. Gandhi taught the people of India—and the people of the world—how to resist violence without being violent. He often was put in jail because his peaceful power threatened the government that ruled his country unfairly.

When you learn about Mahatma Gandhi's life, you will see what makes him amazing. He showed people how to bring about change through peaceful ways. The children of India called him "Bapuji," which means "father." He is known as the father of modern India.

3

Gandhi's Big Family

One day a man from another country went to visit Mahatma Gandhi in India.

Politely the man asked, "How is your family?"

"All of India is my family," Bapuji replied.

And he meant it.

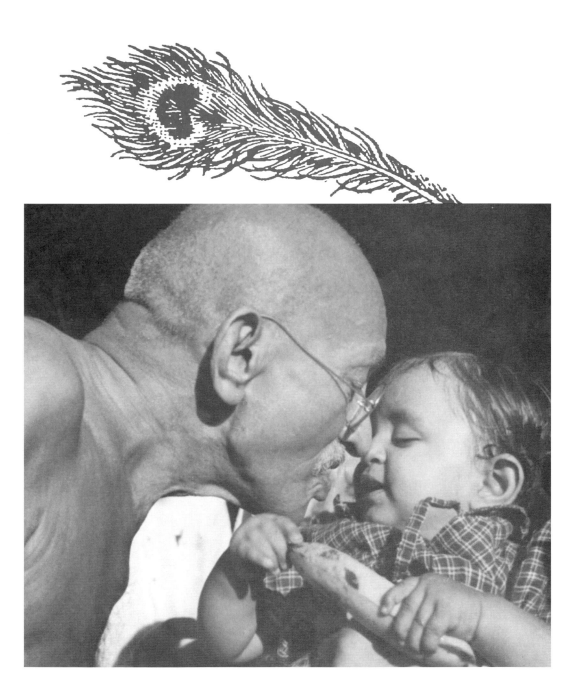

Gandhi's Early Life

When Gandhi was a young boy, he was called by his first name, Mohandas. He grew up in a loving Indian family. His father earned enough money to own a house and provide food for his children to eat every day. Many millions of people who lived in India were not so lucky. Hunger and poverty were common, and many people could not even read. The villagers who used to earn their living by spinning and weaving cotton cloth in their homes had been put out of work. Cheaper cloth could be made by machines in England.

Gandhi as a young lawyer, dressed in British clothing.

When Gandhi returned from England, where he had studied to become a lawyer, he saw that the Indian people had forgotten their proud history. They were powerless under the rule of the British Empire. Gandhi dreamed of India's independence from England, but he was opposed to violence and bloodshed. So he found a way to make things happen peacefully. Gandhi named his way of peaceful change *satyagraha*, which comes from ancient Hindi words meaning "truth and love" and "acting with firmness." *Satyagraha* is often called "Soul-Force."

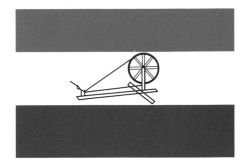

An early design for the Indian National Congress flag.

To help Indian families earn money to live, Gandhi began to teach people to spin thread again in their homes. He used the traditional Indian spinning wheel, called a *charka*, and every day he spent at least half an hour spinning. If everyone followed his example, he said, then all of India would be able to have the basic needs of life. Gandhi worked not for himself but for the people of India. And during the peaceful struggle for Indian freedom, the *charka* was at the center of Gandhi's handspun *satyagraha* flag.

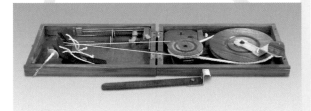

The Indian spinning wheel called a *charka*, which spins thread from cotton grown in local fields.

The Work of a Great Soul

As a young lawyer, Gandhi went to South Africa to help the Indian people who lived there to gain their rights as equal citizens. It was the first time he used his plan of peaceful action, *satyagraha*, and it succeeded. When he returned to India, he was given the title *Mahatma*, which means "Great Soul." But his work in India was only beginning.

Over the years Gandhi traveled all over the Indian continent, wearing the white cotton clothing he had made himself. He taught people about nonviolence (called *ahimsa*) and saw the good in every person. Bapuji's love for people, even people that others thought were "bad," helped them to respond in loving and generous ways themselves.

On the banks of a river at Sabarmati, Gandhi built an ashram, a community where families could live according to their Hindu tradition. It was a peaceful place. Cows and water buffalo cooled themselves in the river as women washed laundry on the banks. Bapuji told stories to the children who followed him everywhere, and he made funny faces to make them laugh.

Peaceful Resistance—Making Salt

People began to see "Soul-Force" in action and began to believe that peaceful resistance could succeed. In 1930 Gandhi decided to show the world how powerful a single act of peaceful resistance could be. He planned to break the British law against Indians making their own salt from seawater. The British government had made a lot of money by charging a tax on salt and all Indians were required to pay it. Gandhi and many of his friends marched 240 miles from the Satyagraha Ashram to the sea. There on the beach Gandhi committed a crime—he picked up a lump of raw sea salt in his hand. Soon people all over India were making their own salt as a peaceful protest. Many thousands were arrested, including Bapuji, but the protest encouraged the Indians to dream of freedom.

A photo taken while Gandhi was in London.

Changing the World

Slowly, firmly, patiently, Mahatma Gandhi was changing India and changing the world. He was one of the most powerful people on earth.

The year after the Salt March, Gandhi was invited to have tea at Buckingham Palace in London with King George V and Queen Mary. He arrived at the palace wearing only a loincloth, sandals, and a shawl, which he had woven himself from thread he had made on his own spinning wheel. He wore his big eyeglasses and a dangling watch. King George met him dressed in fine clothing, with gold medals and ribbons on his chest. He looked like the king of a mighty empire.

Someone later asked Gandhi if he thought that he had worn too little clothing to the fancy tea party. "The King had enough on for both of us," he said.

Now It's Your Turn
SALT AND AIR FOR EVERYONE

When you read about Gandhi's Salt March, you might wonder why he cared so much about ordinary salt. You probably have a salt shaker in the kitchen, and a box of salt in the cabinet. Maybe you've even mixed up some salt and flour and water to make salt dough that you could shape and dry. But in the tropical parts of India, people need salt every day so they can work hard in the hot sun. When they sweat, they use up a lot of the salt in their bodies.

Gandhi believed that it was wrong to charge the poor Indian workers a lot of money for the salt that they could make for free from the saltwater in the ocean. It was a necessity of life.

What might be a necessity of life for you? The air you breathe? The water you drink? What if someone passed a law that said you had to pay a quarter each time you took a deep breath of air? How would you feel?

Make believe that such a law existed and make a plan about what you could do to change the law. You could draw a poster that shows how important it is for people to have free air. You could write a letter to a pretend newspaper explaining that the law is unfair.

Find out how many times a day the average person takes a breath. At twenty-five cents for each breath, how much would it cost to breathe each day? Would people with more money be able to breathe more than poorer people would?

Freedom for Everyone

During Gandhi's lifetime, most of the people in India were members of the Hindu religion, although a great number were Muslims. These two groups fought violently with one another.

In addition to religious divisions, the people of India were also divided by the caste (the level in society) into which they were born.

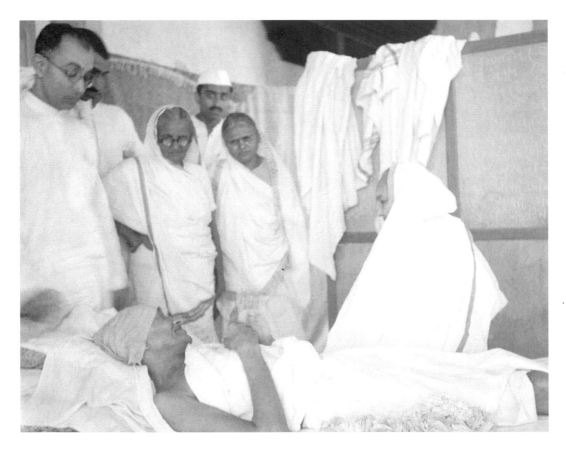

Gandhi feeling weak during one of his fasts.

Families of higher caste had more opportunities and better jobs. They lived more comfortable lives than those of lower caste. And the poorest people, called "untouchables," had no caste at all. They did the dirtiest work and were not even allowed to walk on the public roads.

Gandhi decided to fast, which means that he refused to eat, until the "untouchables" were allowed to live as ordinary citizens instead of as outcasts. When Gandhi fasted, he drank only water and ate no food. He became very weak and often seemed close to dying. But he offered his suffering to God in the hope that his good intentions would soften the hearts of the people who opposed his views. Gandhi's efforts led to equality for Indians of all castes.

Loving All Creation

Gandhi believed that one of the most important gifts of Hinduism to the world was the protection of cows. In India, cows are seen as God's special creatures, and they are allowed to wander freely through the villages and fields. Protecting the cows reminds us that we are all part of one world. Every being that lives is part of Creation and deserves our respect and tender care.

Loving all creatures was not always easy, even for Bapuji. Wild monkeys raided the gardens at the ashram and stole the food that was meant to feed the families. When some people wanted to shoot the monkeys, Bapuji refused to give permission. He did allow them to chase the monkeys away by making noise with big sticks—but never to hit them.

Gandhi's Final Years

For demanding that the British leave India and allow the Indians to govern themselves, Gandhi was put in jail again and again. But in 1947, *satyagraha* won out. India became an independent nation. Gandhi's great sorrow was that he had not been able to bring about peace between the Hindus in India and the Indian Muslims who formed the new nation of Pakistan. Perhaps if he had lived longer, Gandhi might have done so.

Gandhi explains his ideas for peace to Muslims in India.

In 1948 Mahatma Gandhi, India's Great Soul, was killed by a young Hindu man who opposed his desire for equal treatment of Muslims. Almost one million people came to his funeral, and the United Nations ordered its flag to be flown at half-mast in mourning. Gandhi had inspired the world.

Fascinating Fact

When Gandhi died in 1948, his only worldly possessions were two pair of sandals, his watch and glasses, bowls, spoons, and a book of songs.

An Amazing Life

Mahatma Gandhi began his work as a young Hindu lawyer in India, and through his deep belief in peaceful protest against injustice, he became a world leader and an inspiration to people such as Martin Luther King Jr. Isn't that amazing?

23

Meeting with Indian Prime Minister Jawaharlal Nehru.

Gandhi's Beliefs

Bapuji believed with all his heart that every good action and thought in our day could help to make the world a better place.

He said, "God whispered into my ears, 'Nothing great could be achieved unless one cares for the smallest thing.' God hangs the greatest weight on the smallest pegs."

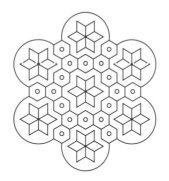

Now It's Your Turn

CARING FOR THE SMALLEST THING

 When you have a new box of colored chalk, are you eager to draw on the chalkboard or on the sidewalk? Do you love to open a brand-new box of crayons? When the stick of chalk wears down to just a little stub, or the crayon breaks in half, what do you do with it?

Do you throw away the crayon or the piece of chalk, thinking it's too small to be of any use?

Gandhi said that it was an act of violence against the environment to throw away anything that could still be used. Precious resources were used to make that chalk or that crayon. If we waste resources, then people will have even less of what they need.

What could you do with the crayon pieces? *With a grownup's help,* you could melt the pieces back into wax and make a new mixed-up-color crayon or a candle. You could hold the piece of chalk sideways and use it to make a thick line or color a part of your picture. How about using many colors in small amounts to draw your picture, instead of one new stick of a single color?

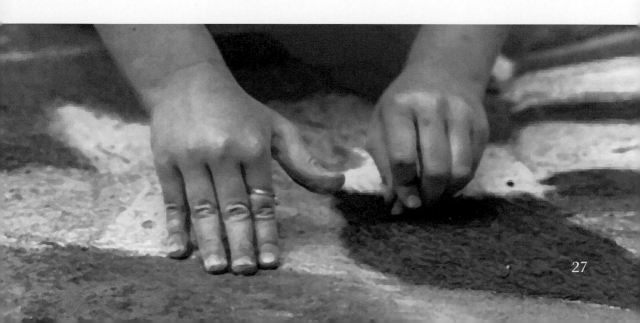

Now It's Your Turn

WHAT DO YOU REALLY NEED?

Gandhi lived a simple life. He owned only what he needed. He dressed in the handmade clothes of a poor Indian. Because he was not worried about taking care of many possessions, he could devote his time and energy to making life better for other people.

On a big sheet of paper, make a list of all the things you own. It might be a long list. Maybe you have seven shirts and three sweaters. Maybe you have twelve picture books. Maybe you have two bicycles, if you count the old one that you've outgrown.

Now draw a circle around the things that you really need. Draw a line through everything you own that you could live without. Are there more circles or more lines? Can you make the number of circles smaller? How about giving that old small bicycle to a younger child who could use it? Are there any "baby" books that you might want to give to a daycare center or nursery school?

Important Events in the Life of Mahatma Gandhi

1888—As a Hindu law student in London, Gandhi began to read about Christians, Buddhists, and Muslims to understand other religious traditions.

1892—While in South Africa he became a leader of the movement to help stop racial prejudice against Indians who lived there.

1906—Gandhi developed the idea of active, peaceful resistance, which he called *satyagraha*, for the Indians to use in their struggle for equal rights as citizens of the British Empire.

1914—After a law was passed to give equality to Indians living in South Africa, Gandhi returned to India to work for *swaraj*, which means the right of Indians to govern themselves.

1918—Gandhi helped Indian textile mill workers in their strike for better wages by encouraging nonviolent protest and fasting.

1920s—Gandhi quietly worked to inspire the Indian people to achieve independence from British rule and was often arrested.

1930—Gandhi united the Indian people behind him in a protest of the British tax on salt, using *satyagraha*.

1932—Gandhi fasted to protest the idea of certain people being treated as "untouchables." His action led to political equality for the poorest people.

1942—His demand for Indian independence made Gandhi such a threat to the British government that he was jailed for two years.

1947—Gandhi's dream of Indian independence was fulfilled, but Gandhi was saddened because the country was divided into two separate nations—India for the Hindus and Pakistan for the Muslims.

1948—Gandhi was killed by a man who did not agree with his desire for equal treatment of people of all religions.

Important Words to Know

Ashram A community where people live according to their religious tradition and under the guidance of a spiritual teacher.

British Empire The group of countries around the world that were colonies or territories under the rule of the British government in England, which in 1914 extended over one fifth of the earth's available land and over one quarter of its population.

Caste system The division of Indian society into different levels, called castes, depending on family and occupation.

Hindu A member of one of the world's major religions, founded in India many centuries ago.

Mahatma A word that means "Great Soul" in Hindi, a language spoken in India.

Muslim A person who practices the religious faith of Islam, founded by the Prophet Muhammad nearly 1,500 years ago.

Racial prejudice Treating people differently, usually in unfair ways, because of the color of their skin.

Satyagraha Gandhi's word for making things happen peacefully, which he created from the ancient Hindi words for "truth and love" and "acting with firmness."

Untouchables A group of people in India who did the lowliest work and were considered unclean because they were outside the caste system.

Gandhi: India's Great Soul

2004 First Printing
Text © 2004 by SkyLight Paths Publishing
Illustrations © 2002 by Stephen Marchesi

Library of Congress Cataloging-in-Publication Data
Shaw, Maura D.
Gandhi, India's great soul / by Maura D. Shaw ; illustrations by Stephen Marchesi.
p. cm.–(Spiritual biographies for young readers)
Summary: A biography of Mahatma Gandhi which emphasizes the spiritual beliefs that guided his actions in the nonviolent battle to secure India's independence from Great Britain. Includes activities and a note for parents and teachers.
ISBN 1-893361-91-8
1. Gandhi, Mahatma, 1869–1948–Juvenile literature. 2. Statesmen–India–Biography–Juvenile literature. 3. Nationalists–India–Biography–Juvenile literature. [1. Gandhi, Mahatma, 1869–1948. 2. Statesmen. 3. India–Politics and government–1919–1947.] I. Marchesi, Stephen, ill. II. Title. III. Series.
DS481.G3 S4795 2003
954.03'5'092–dc22
                                                                                          2003011814

10 9 8 7 6 5 4 3 2 1
Manufactured in Hong Kong

A special thank you to Shelly Angers for her help in creating the activities in this book.

Grateful acknowledgment is given for permission to reprint material belonging to Arun Gandhi and The M. K. Gandhi Institute for Nonviolence (www.gandhiinstitute.org). The Charka photo on page 7 is reprinted courtesy of The Woolery, P.O. Box 468, Murfreesboro, NC 27855, 1-800-441-9665, www.woolery.com. Some additional images © Clipart.com.

Special thanks for permission to reprint the photographs in this book is extended to GandhiServe—a charitable foundation aiming to promote the life and work of Mahatma Gandhi, believing firmly that Gandhi's message of truth, love, and nonviolence is more relevant than ever before. In addition to providing educational programs, GandhiServe Foundation works to safeguard and distribute documents, photographs, and films relating to Gandhi and the Indian independence movement. Its archive is the largest of its kind outside India and, along with further details about the foundation, can be viewed online at gandhiserve.org.

Every effort has been made to trace and acknowledge copyright holders of all material used in this book. The publisher apologizes for any errors or omissions that may remain, and asks that any omissions be brought to their attention so they may be corrected in future editions.

Walking Together, Finding the Way
Published by SkyLight Paths Publishing
A Division of LongHill Partners, Inc.
Sunset Farm Offices, Route 4, P.O. Box 237
Woodstock, VT 05091
Tel: (802) 457-4000   Fax: (802) 457-4004
www.skylightpaths.com